Resilience:
Navigating Loss
in a Time of Crisis

Resilience:
Navigating Loss
in a Time of Crisis

Jules De Vitto

CHANGEMAKERS
BOOKS

Winchester, UK
Washington, USA

JOHN HUNT PUBLISHING

First published by Changemakers Books, 2020
Changemakers Books is an imprint of John Hunt Publishing Ltd., No. 3 East Street,
Alresford, Hampshire SO24 9EE, UK
office@jhpbooks.com
www.johnhuntpublishing.com
www.changemakers-books.com

For distributor details and how to order please visit the 'Ordering' section on our website.

ISBN: 978 1 78904 699 1
978 1 78904 700 4 (ebook)
Library of Congress Control Number: 00000000

A CIP catalogue record for this book is available from the British Library.

Design: Stuart Davies

UK: Printed and bound by CPI Group (UK) Ltd, Croydon, CR0 4YY
Printed in North America by CPI GPS partners

We operate a distinctive and ethical publishing philosophy in
all areas of our business, from our global network of authors to
production and worldwide distribution.

Contents

Preface

I wrote this book amid the coronavirus pandemic in April 2020. It was a synchronous moment, in which Tim Ward, Publisher of Changemaker Books contacted me about the publications of the resilience series - a selection of books to support people through times of crisis. The contents of this book came together as a result of my work as a transpersonal coach and therapist along with the experiences, insights and reflections I had formed through my own journey of loss, change and transition that I have experienced, specifically, over the two years prior to the manifestation of this book.

The universality of loss and grief that came to be experienced by so many during the coronavirus pandemic of 2019-2020 propelled me to write this book. I have brought in my passion for transpersonal psychology as well as the integration of spiritual insights and mindfulness practices. It is my hope that this book will help those who have experienced any form of loss to cultivate resilience, courage and strength through their times of struggle.

It is my experiences that a time of crisis and loss can 'break us open' and it is the most difficult periods in our lives which leads to our ultimate growth and transformation. I believe that our journey through grief and uncertainty needs to be navigated slowly, with presence and our emotions require a compassionate holding along the path. I write briefly about my Grandfather and the sharing of his incredible story as a prisoner of war. This story serves as a reminder of how we can find courage and purpose no matter how difficult our experiences are. It also reminds us about the significance of connection and coming together as a community in times of crisis.

Acknowledgments

Many thanks to Tim Ward, Publisher of Changemakers Books for granting me this opportunity to write *Resilience: Navigating Loss in a Time of Crisis* and contribute towards the Resilience Series, which has been put together to help people through the coronavirus pandemic, and future crises. I am honored to be a part of this series of books and I'd also like to thank John Hunt, owner and publishing manager of the Resilience Series, whose idea it was to publish this series of books in a very short and record period of time! Thank you to my very loyal friends who, from a distance and while in 'lockdown', still encouraged and supported me, or took the time to read my draft in the short weeks leading up to the publication of this book.

Foreword: *Resilience in a Time of Crisis*

"What can we do to help?"

In a time of crisis - such as the 2020 COVID-19 pandemic - we all have a natural impulse to help our neighbors. John Hunt, founder of John Hunt Publishing, asked this question of our company, and then offered a suggestion. He proposed producing a series of short books written by experts offering practical, emotional, and spiritual skills to help people survive in the midst of a crisis.

To reach people when they need it most, John wanted to accomplish this in forty days. Bear in mind, the normal process of bringing a book from concept to market takes at least eighteen months. As publisher of the JHP imprint Changemakers Books, I volunteered to execute this audacious plan. My imprint publishes books about personal and social transformation, and I already knew many authors with exactly the kinds of expertise we needed. That's how the *Resilience Series* was born.

I was overwhelmed by my authors' responses. Ten of them immediately said yes and agreed to the impossible deadline. The book you hold in your hands is the result of this intensive, collaborative effort. On behalf of John, myself, the authors and production team, our intention for you is that you take to heart the skills and techniques offered to you in these pages. Master them. Make yourself stronger. Share your newfound resilience with those around you. Together, we can not only survive, but learn how to thrive in tough times. By so doing, we can find our way to a better future.

Tim Ward
Publisher, Changemakers Books
May 1, 2020

Introduction

This book offers a space in which to acknowledge the profound impact that loss can have on us. Many of us will be forced to grieve significant losses such as the death of loved ones, and these are the losses which will undoubtedly have a lasting impact on us all. We will also explore the other forms of loss and grief which many of us will experience through times of crisis. When a business we worked hard to build is brought to a halt, or our financial security is compromised, we have experienced loss. When our freedom has been restricted and we can no longer visit our family or our elders, that we fear we will soon lose, we experience grief. When we intellectualize that at some point our lives will return to 'normal' but intuitively know that things will never be quite the same 'normal' again, we experience uncertainty and fear. When the deeper, existential questions of what gives us meaning and purpose are brought to the surface and we wonder how we'll find the resilience to move forward and re-build our lives, we experience moments of despair.

Within this book we will discover the various forms of loss and explore the psychological impact of these losses; honoring the process of grief that follows. I will offer practices which guide us through this process, such as offering greater compassion for ourselves and opening space for all the emotions that arise in the face of uncertainty. When navigating loss and grief our worldview and belief systems are often shattered. Our fragility is unveiled, yet, within this space of instability and vulnerability we are offered a tremendous opportunity to go inwards, to re-define what gives us meaning and purpose and to offer gratitude for all that is important to us. We will explore how times of crisis can provide a deeper connection with our authentic selves and with the sacred. We will learn to embrace our vulnerability, finding acceptance and the bravery to surrender to the impermanence of life and to the process of endings and renewal.

When news of COVID-19 entered our lives in the late months of 2019, none of us were prepared for the sudden onset of the global crisis that followed. We watched as China suffered the tragic deaths of thousands and experienced the loss of their freedom as millions of people entered lockdown in the city of Wuhan and surrounding provinces. Months of uncertainty, experiences of loss and grief followed, and the Chinese offered songs of hope and encouragement to each other from the confinements of their balconies.

I had a close relationship with China; Shanghai had been my home for six years, from 2012 until 2018, and I felt deeply connected to their culture and country. My heart went out to those affected by this extraordinary crisis and now in London, I watched from a distance with the rest of the world, not knowing that the same fate would soon enter our lives and impact us in unprecedented ways. The questions we asked of China, their county and their people became our own. It went from a terrifying ordeal that was being experienced by some, to a global issue being faced by so many around the world. It became a matter of unity and 'we're all in this together' was a phrase commonly spread across social media in the months that followed. As COVID-19 crossed borders into England in the early months of 2020, many of us were consumed with fear; we wondered what impact the virus would have on us and the rest of the world, and how we would navigate the uncertainty that followed.

When I left China in the summer of 2018, I embarked on a significant journey of transition and transformation. I chose to leave my home, friendships, a familiar structure, a lifelong career, a culture I'd grown accustomed to and huge parts of my identity behind. This was the beginning of a long journey filled with new and exciting opportunities for travel and work. Yet, I also traversed many forms of loss and an unexpected process of grief and renewal that came with these losses. I navigated a significant amount of uncertainty in which many people, places and relationships entered my life and then left again. It felt like I became somewhat of an expert on what it meant to go through change and transition and the synchronicities I encountered, the lessons I was presented with, were too many to count. When I stepped into the unknown, I learnt the art of letting go, of falling and pulling myself back up again. When the COVID-19 crisis emerged, I was just beginning to 'settle' into a new life in London, but it seemed that there was an alternative plan in store for all of us. My life was thrown into another bout of uncertainty: a business I had been working hard to build, a part-time job and financial security was pulled abruptly from under me. The dreams I had and the plans I'd made, the friendships and the life I was just settling into was ground to a halt. News of a relative passing due to the virus, the acknowledgment that the following months would be spent in almost complete 'isolation', all hit within the space of a week. The impact of the virus and the realities of loss and endings, witnessing the shattered dreams of many people around me, the uncertainty of it all and the way change can arrive, and loss can consume people in an instance, became all too real. I was met with denial, fear, frustration and anxiety; an accumulation of disappointment and a resistance to move through any more uncertainty.

Yet, in the days that followed, deep in meditation and in a split moment of introspection, I connected with the awareness that we are more resilient than we ever imagine ourselves to be. It reminded me of the tremendous possibilities that emerge in moments of crisis. The potential that arises from a space of uncertainty and what happens when we find the courage to grieve our losses and to navigate waves of the unknown. When everything seemingly crumbles and we are granted with the opportunity to re-build our lives from another - unexpected space, there can arise an unlimited number of opportunities. So, the lessons and experiences I'd written about over the past 18 months, which I had stored in a blue file on my laptop, the one's of: transition, change, crisis, loss and recovery suddenly seemed to serve a purpose and which I share throughout this book.

Chapter 1

Resilience

What is Resilience?

"The greatest glory in living lies not in never falling, but in rising every time we fall"
Nelson Mandela

The word 'resilience' comes from the Latin word 'resilio' which means 'to bounce back' or retaliate. Emotional resilience is our ability to cope with trauma, threats or significant sources of stress while maintaining a healthy level of psychological and physical functioning. For those of us who have experienced sudden losses, we feel fragile, broken and our belief in a safe and secure world is often compromised. It can feel like the ground below us has shaken and the foundations that kept things together have collapsed.

Two months before we entered, what became known as 'lockdown', I had a vivid and significant dream. In the dream, I stood watching a storm in which dark clouds encroached and occupied the skyline. In the distance a strong, powerful bolt of lightning stuck an unrecognizable, but sturdy building, which proceeded to catch fire. The building collapsed from the force of the lightning and the fire that engulfed it. The fire quickly descended into the surrounding village and the land beyond it. The people's faces drowned with fear, they turned and fled in their masses. I also ran from the fire, but as I did, I witnessed a group of people working together and collecting barrels of water in an attempt to stop the fire from spreading. In that moment, I chose to stay and help the people with the water. It was months later, in the midst of the pandemic, that I came to understand the significance of this dream. As I reflect on it now, I am struck by the importance of the people with the barrels of water and my choice to stay with them. Water is symbolic of our emotions, and it seemed that those who stayed, were choosing resilience and the courage to work with the energy of their emotions, to transform fear and to turn towards chaos and uncertainty – instead of running away from it.

The symbolism in my dream is also characteristic of the archetypal image that is shared through the tower card in the Tarot Deck. Carl Jung spoke about how Tarot offers insight into the full spectrum of human archetypes and can be used as an analytical tool for our emotions. The cards offer symbols and images which represent the common myths that play out in our lives and when such images are presented to us; they are offering us the chance to bring what can lie in the unconscious into conscious awareness. They can also offer guidance, or an alternative perspective to situations – which may be particularly helpful as we navigate challenging circumstances. The reason I share my dream and its connection to the tower card is because they teach us about choice and about the positive potential of destruction and chaos.

The image on the tower card shows a black, cloud ridden sky, in which a bolt of lightning strikes the crown of a tower. Those inside the tower fall and the image summons up emotions of destruction, death, falling and failure. The card expresses the sudden downfall of materialism and of the ego; a collapsing of the very foundations which hold us. As harrowing as the image on the card looks and with the warning of impending difficulty, struggle and upheaval – the collapsing of the tower also suggests that what follows will be a time of significant spiritual growth and awakening that leads to the reconstruction of ourselves and of humanity. I wonder how much this relates to the experience of going through a global pandemic? Can a crisis like this be a time of spiritual and psychological emergence? Is it an opportunity for us to re-evaluate what is important to us and see what can arise from the space of loss, chaos and uncertainty? It seems there is a huge amount of potential for positive transformation to take place, when so much is lost and a space emerges from what we have lost. Within this book I will offer practices and suggestions on how we can cultivate the strength to move resiliently into this space.

What *usually* builds our Resilience?

As mentioned, resilience is a choice we make, and it is something that can be cultivated over time. It isn't something that some people have, and others don't but it is a process which can be maintained through consistent and conscious practices. Fostering resilience requires us to: connect with a purpose for cultivating it in the first place, setting the intention to do it and then taking specific actions which continue to nurture a healthy mind, body and spirit.

It is also important to note that resilience isn't always about actively 'doing' and it's not about forcing our process, nor is it about putting on a hard exterior that tells the world we are always 'strong'. It isn't the belief that 'we can get through anything' or that 'we cannot be broken' – it is the contrast of this. It is the moments where we embrace our vulnerability and we surrender to our brokenness that we can connect with our more authentic and humble self. From this self, we are gifted with the choice to find strength, courage and faith to move forward with our journey.

Resilience is an interplay between *doing* and *being* and integrating the masculine and feminine polarities of our selves. This means that while we are consciously taking action to engage in practices that cultivate a resilient attitude, we are also entering a place of *being* where we embrace the totality of our experience and find acceptance for all that arises, regardless of whether we label it as *good* or *bad*.

We maintain resilience through a combination of internal and external factors. This includes the routines, practices and structures that we have in place to support us, our connection with community and how much we engage in healthy relationships with others. We are likely to feel more resilient to loss, when we have caring and supportive relationships, a network of friends and family and a knowing that we belong to something greater than ourselves. As well as our connection with friends and family, a connection to Earth, nature and our environment is crucial. Evidence has shown that being in nature reduces anger, stress and fear and it increases positive emotions such as feeling calm, peaceful and happy. Engaging in acts of self-care and focusing on things like diet and exercise are also found to promote resilience and maintain a healthy body and mind. Self-care is also connected to an ability to be compassionate for our emotional experiences and hold space for them.

Our level of resilience will depend on our worldview, how we understand the fundamental nature of the universe and the perspectives that are tied into our deeply held belief systems. Some of us will have strong spiritual beliefs and trust in a greater intelligence, enabling us to step into a place of surrender, more readily, in times of crisis. For some of us, it is times of crisis than compromise our spiritual beliefs and cause us to re-evaluate or move away from them entirely. It is likely that many of us will question our core beliefs during challenging times so our resilience will include how much we're able to the manage shifts made to our deeply held beliefs and values. How well we can do this will depend on our level of self-awareness, an ability to observe our thought processes and our level of cognitive flexibility. Just like exercising or going to the gym to build muscle, we need to make a commitment to the cultivation of mental strength and flexibility and in this book, we will explore how this commitment is made when going through immense periods of loss and adversity.

Resilience during times of Crisis

When going through times of crisis, many of the protective factors which contribute towards our level of resilience are compromised. In this book, I talk specifically about the loss and uncertainty that has occurred as a result of the coronavirus pandemic, but the process of grief and the practices I suggest to support us through these difficult times, can also be applied to many other forms of crisis or difficulties.

The coronavirus pandemic has meant that our usual routines which involve going to the office and connecting with colleagues; being a member of a community; going to networking events; visiting places of worship; meeting friends for dinner; nights out; weekends away and holidays have been temporarily removed from our lives. The uncertainty and the not knowing when we will take part in these routines and communities again, only adds to our anxiety. For many of us, connecting with nature is very difficult right now as we are only allowed a daily walk in the park and for some, this is not even an option. These restrictions which have been placed on our freedom can have a very detrimental effect on our psychological and physical health. In chapters 3, 4 and 5 I will suggest practices which will help cultivate resilience, meanwhile stepping into a space of surrender (this is different from giving up!). First, we will dive deeper into the various forms of loss and what our emotional landscape may look like during this time.

Chapter 2

Loss and Endings

"New beginnings are often disguised as painful endings"
Lao Tzu.

The endings and losses that have entrenched the lives of so many due to the global COVID-19 crisis, are pervasive – they have been experienced in numerous ways and in various magnitudes. There are the primary losses of lives, the deaths of thousands of people and our loved ones. These losses and the grief that follows is unfathomable and we will be required to navigate this process with great compassion and courage. Yet, it is also important for us to acknowledge the losses that go beyond bereavement. This includes the material losses of businesses, jobs, offices, school communities, relationships and marriages which have been broken due the pressures of the crisis. There is the loss of routines and structures which formed the foundation of our day-to-day lives; the loss of financial security and the fears that the threat of financial uncertainty brings to so many of us. Some of us have experienced the loss of hope because the dreams of the life we wanted to live have been suddenly snatched from us. Many of us have lost the freedom to engage in meaningful actives and the roles that were instrumental in forming our very identity. We have also lost the labels we were given and so we may ask 'who am I if I am not...?' These existential questions are some of the most difficult questions we can ever face and impact us on a deep psychology, emotional and spiritual level.

As difficult as these losses are, they can also ignite a search in us which connects us to a deeper part of ourselves. It is a process of breaking open just like the emergence out of a cocoon, these painful losses become the catalyst for a significant stage of our lives: an opportunity for growth and transformation. Abraham Maslow said that throughout life, we are faced with an ongoing series of choices between safety and growth. What many of us have experienced with the onset of the pandemic, is an abrupt pause, a sudden closing of businesses or schools and incomplete projects. Some have a sign over them saying, 'back in a few months', others have been closed indefinitely or have reluctantly been thrown away. Many things are waiting, simply left with a question mark. So, we have a choice as to whether we remain 'frozen in time' and stuck with the frustration of the indefinite losses, or whether we take manageable steps forward, moving into growth and expansion with a brand-new perspective. We are called to remember the phrase we all know so well, 'as one door closes, many more open'.

Grief

"The wound is uncovered, so it can be worked with. Sometimes we do this consciously, but more often, life simply breaks us open"
Mariana Caplan

Grief is a psychological, emotional and spiritual response to significant loss and the intensity of it can consume us. It includes the awakening of powerful emotions such as despair, anger, denial, depression and for many an onset of hopelessness. Other emotions which we will run into on our pathway through grief include feeling sad, shocked, numb, stressed, anxious and confused.

The grief that is experienced when a number of losses occur in a short space of time or consecutively – one after the other, can be profound. This is likely to be the case for many people experiencing the current pandemic. These consecutive losses can leave wounds that if left hidden, are carried around for months, years or even decades – just waiting to be healed.

It is the accumulation of this unacknowledged grief that can push many of us into moments of despair. Yet, it is in those moments of despair, where we will be given a choice, to either step away from the grief or to step into it and surrender. It is this point of surrender which enables us to lean into our suffering with courage and strength and it is the journey we embark on from this point that will become so crucial.

This act of leaning into our grief in this way, is vital because if we don't, we are in danger of living somewhere in an abyss of the 'in-between'. This is where we turn away from our grief and the pain of loss and at the same time refuse to open our hearts fully to the potential of genuine love. So, we feel everything, but nothing completely and we only scratch the surface of what it means to be alive. We numb ourselves, avoid and deny the depths of our feelings and our soul's very calling.

It is likely that we're all experiencing some form of anticipatory grief in knowing that there's a possibility of our loved ones becoming ill or even dying amidst the crisis. When the reality of something we are so afraid of is so close to home, we can undoubtedly experience a huge amount of anxiety about it. We wonder how we can keep those who are close to us and those who are vulnerable safe. When the numbers of those who have died are presented to us on our TV screens, it is hard to grasp the reality of those statistics and of the number of lives that have been affected. The reality is, death is not something we can escape and perhaps the inevitable cycle of life and death is something we are being propelled to look at more closely throughout this pandemic.

There will also be anticipatory grief surrounding financial issues and the uncertainty of the businesses or homes we own. Will our financial security or the careers that we have spent a lifetime working in, still be there for us when the crisis is over? We may also feel anticipation surrounding other types of relationships – will our marriage withstand this crisis and the pressures of spending so much time together? On the other hand, some of us might ask, will my relationship pull through the many months we have had to spend apart during the isolation?

Stages of Grief

Elisabeth Kübler-Ross first proposed the five stages of grief in her 1969 book *On Death and Dying*. It is important to note that these stages are a framework for understanding the process of grief, but grief is actually a messy process, it is not linear, and it is different for everyone. When going through crisis, it is likely that our experiences of grief are going to vary greatly because of the wide range of losses that are experienced. We can't place our losses and the process of grief into a specific category; however, I find these stages to be a helpful road map for those who want to understand their journey more fully. The original five stages are: Denial, Anger, Bargaining, Depression and Acceptance. Since then a sixth stage has been added which is finding meaning. The topic of finding meaning and purpose in times of crisis is something I will go into, in much more detail, in chapter 6 of this book.

Denial: When we are in denial, we can feel paralyzed or experience a sense of numbness. This might have happened when we were told that we were entering lockdown, when the schools closed or when we realized we were not going to be able to see our friends and family again for an (unknown) period of time. Denial is an important protective mechanism as we move through the shock of loss. We are only letting in as much as we can handle at this point and this helps us to manage our emotions on an unconscious level.

Anger: We will encounter many forms of emotions, however, usually at the fore-front of these emotions is anger or irritability.

There will be anger at the fact that we have had to suddenly put many aspects of our lives on hold, anger that we can't visit loved ones who might get sick. We are angry that our children may not go to school and our freedom has been seized from us. We will be angry if we lose our loved ones before their time. Feeling angry is a natural part of the process and it is important to get to know it, just as we will talk about it in further sections of this book – we welcome all emotions including the emotions of anger – without judging them. It is usually this anger which is masking our underlying pain or sadness and the reality that a part of our life has been put on hold or has in fact, ended. Another form of anger may be anger towards a higher power which we perceive has abandoned us in a time of need, we are bitter that life can be so unfair and we may even want to push those we love away from us as we process our anger.

Bargaining: During this stage, we are desperate for things to go back to how they were before this crisis hit. We ask, 'what if' or 'if only'. It is an attempt for us to bring order back to chaos because we don't want to go through this pain and loss anymore. We may daydream about life before the lockdown, or before our loved ones became ill and passed away, we may wonder if there was anything we could have done to have kept them safe. We may question if there is another reality that exists, where this is not happening. We wonder about the future, when this is over – can we bring back the things and the people we have lost? Can we have our lives go back to normal again? This will be the lived experience for many, who seek to negotiate an alternative reality and fantasize about a different life – the one we had before or the one that will come when this crisis is over.

Depression: It is normal to experience depression as we move through our journey. We can go through a deep sense of emptiness and loneliness when we experience this unknown stage of our lives. This depression and sense of loneliness is a normal response to the losses we have encountered, it is part of the healing process and it will take time to move through. Depression is often diagnosed as an "illness" something to be treated through medication and "recover" from. As a result, we often try to avoid or move away from any discomfort we encounter. This may be with the use of medication or distracting ourselves from our pain and just like with anger, we need to embrace experiences of depression and accept them. I will go into depression in more detail in chapter 6.

Acceptance: Acceptance is where we step into our new reality, we learn to live with it, to not try to change anything or to move back to how it was before. We start to feel better about the situation and move towards a gentler acceptance for the reality of our new life. We begin to consider how to move forward and what this new stage of our existence will bring for us. This doesn't mean we will ever forget our loved ones who have passed away or the parts of our life that brought us so much joy in the past, but we can now take small steps forward into a new way of being.

To accept our situation means to bring awareness to our emotions, hold space for them and then welcome them into us with self-compassion. This enables us to relax into these emotions and enter a more expansive, peaceful space. So the letting go is a welcoming of everything and then finding the ability to move forward based on a more coherent and loving energy. In the next part we will go into more detail, the specific practices which can be used for working through experiences of loss and navigating the uncertainty that follows.

The well-mapped stages of grief are a beautiful resource to make sense of our experiences. Remember, they are not linear and not everyone will move through them in the same order, or even at all. The losses that have been experienced during this pandemic are multi-dimensional. Some will feel the impact of their losses for the rest of their lives, other losses might be easier to accept and move on from. The important thing is that we recognize there are a variety of emotions that arise as we navigate the journey through loss and grief and our experiences will be different every day. We will speak about this in the following chapters, as it is crucial that we make space for these emotions and we don't try to push them away.

Although it can sound counterintuitive to stay present with difficult emotions (we fear they might be too much to handle) it has been my experience that when we do this, the intensity of them lessens. I notice a huge shift in my ability to work through overpowering emotions when I can stay present with my pain and say "I don't feel okay today, but that's okay."

Society, our friends and family want us to feel healthy and be happy, yet, there is nothing wrong with telling someone you're having a bad day, that you're struggling with your losses. You can do this without becoming a 'victim' to your pain. Remember that the pain of loss and grief is neither good, nor bad but it is a part of our human experience. Authentically listening to our emotions in this way, also teaches us the importance of vulnerability and being able to share our difficulties with each other. Telling someone else you're struggling doesn't mean anyone needs to fix or change anything, but there is so much value in sharing our stories with each other.

Making space for grief is a journey I'm still on. There was a time, I didn't believe I was entitled to feel grief for the losses I'd encountered. I wonder how many of us might feel like that now? Can we acknowledge that our experiences are worthy enough to be held and grieved? When I was 23, I learned how grief consumes you in mysterious ways and what happens when you try to negate or run away from it. I learnt how it can steal your soul, kidnap your dreams and take away the trust that you have in a secure world. As I write this book, with the thoughts of those that are experiencing the loss of loved ones, I'm also reminded that even though some things will inevitably be lost or die, while the pain of grief will remain imprinted on our hearts forever and some dreams may be snatched from us, or get put on hold – the dreams that are meant to be and the people we love, whether they are lost or still alive, will always be with us.

Chapter 3

Cultivating Emotional Awareness

"To stay with that shakiness-to stay with a broken heart, with a rumbling stomach, with the feeling of hopelessness-that is the path of true awakening"
Pema Chodron

When we are bombarded with a range of negative emotions, it is easy for us to try and avoid experiencing them. We find many ways to distract ourselves sometimes by: over-working, eating too much, numbing ourselves through TV or through sex, drugs and alcohol addiction. We try to avoid our emotions because we are afraid that we will be overwhelmed and not able to manage the pain we are experiencing. When we avoid our emotions, they will inevitably find other ways to be expressed; they might emerge as physical pain, tension or an underlying and persistent sense of irritation. This irritation may build up over time, leading us to act in ways that we wouldn't normally, such as displaying aggression and anger towards others. What is crucial here is that we find ways to draw awareness to our emotions and attempt to stay present with them without getting overwhelmed or drowning in them. The mindful practices that I share in the following chapter enable us to do just this, as we learn to be the observer of our emotions and recognize that they are part of our experience but not the whole of who we are. In addition to this, we only work with the emotions that we are ready to at that moment in time, and we approach all our experiences with open, non-judgmental awareness.

Mindfulness Awareness

One of the first things we can practice is cultivating greater awareness for our emotional experiences. The scope of our awareness can be narrow or expanded, it can be scattered and moving between many objects or it can be focused on one object at a time. Our goal is to step into a space where we can become aware of the awareness itself! This is where we discern when and how our attention shifts from one object to the other, or whether our awareness is narrow, expanded, scattered or focused. As we develop our practice, we can then consciously choose to direct our attention to the present moment and also enter an open state of awareness. This expanded state of awareness involves paying attention to what is present in our external environment while simultaneously being aware of what is going on inside our mind and body.

We are not trying to change anything about our experience, nor are we attempting to 'improve' our ability to pay attention to what is going on. This is not the purpose of the mindfulness awareness that we will talk about here. We are simply trying our best to notice, in this moment, what emotions and experiences are present for us. So, the cultivation of mindfulness awareness is particularly important when we're going through intense emotional experiences. No matter how subtle or strong these emotions are, when we learn to bring awareness to the different dimensions of these experiences then we are on the first step towards transforming our response to these states.

Holding Space for our Emotions

How do we hold space for our emotions, without also getting lost in them?

We are learning about the importance of not turning away from our suffering. Mindfulness practices do not involve switching off from our pain or even maintaining a constant state of relaxation and peace. The practice is about connecting more deeply with our emotions and feeling them, in their entirety. This can be challenging, yet when we connect with our sense of aloneness, sadness and pain it enables us to move through our experiences of uncertainty, loss and fear with greater ease and presence. With practice, it is possible to recognize emotions arising in our body, as well as choose how we want to react or respond to those emotions.

All your emotions are experienced on a visceral level in the body and strong emotions may be associated with psychosomatic problems if they are not brought into your conscious awareness. Meditation connects you more deeply with the subtleties of your body so, before you become overwhelmed by an emotion, you notice it arising. When you feel frustrated, you might sense a knot in your stomach or heart area, you might feel tension in your shoulders or a shortness of breath. With emotions like grief or sadness there is often a weight or pressing down on your heart area, a stiff neck or a weakness in the legs. When going through a large amount of anxiety, fear, sadness or other powerful emotions you can apply mindfulness practices to connect with the visceral sense of these emotions in the body, meanwhile – learning to become an observer of your thoughts and the larger narrative of the mind.

Mindfulness Practice

For the purpose of the following practice, bring to mind an emotion that has been coming up a lot for you lately. Don't choose something that is too overwhelming at this point, but an emotion which you would like to try to bring greater awareness to.

Begin this practice by paying particular attention to your breathing. As you are breathing in and out, focus on making the exhalation slightly longer. Next, bring your breath back to a natural pace.

Within this more centered and calm space, bring into your attention the emotion that you have chosen to work on. See if you recognize where the emotion rests in your body. Is there a tightness in your chest or your throat area? Does your body feel heavy or perhaps you even feel disconnected from your body entirely? If this is the case, pay attention to the felt sense of that, and continue to scan your body from head to toe – simply observe what is there.

See if you can visualize a certain shape, size or color in relation to the felt sense in the body. Is there a density or texture to it? It might change shape or size and that's okay, just continue to witness what is arising without trying to control it in any way.

Once we have observed the sensation of the emotion in the body, we also want to observe the mind and the 'story' that is attached to our experience. What thoughts are present as you observe your experience? Are there thoughts that your experience is wrong? Are you trying to push anything away? Do you wish things were different?

Observe these thoughts and see where your mind takes you, what story is being formed about your emotions and who you are? Remember that all your emotions are trying to support you in some way – so ask how this emotion is trying to help you out – what is the fear or anxiety trying to do for you? (Even if it is not being successful at this!) If your mind is overthinking, doubting or questioning, then ask - what is my mind attempting to do by overthinking like this? What is it searching for?

Take a minute to sit with your experience and allow whatever needs to come into your awareness to arise. Now, thank your mind and body for sharing what it has shared with you today. Take three deep breaths, in through your nose and out through your mouth and slowly begin to open your eyes again. Notice how your body and mind feel now compared to the beginning of the practice.

Take a moment to write down or draw any specific images, sensations or words that came to you during the session. Even if these images, sensations or words make little sense to you it is good to keep a record of your experiences. Do this without over-analyzing what your experience was as you might not be able to make complete sense of it right now, but what is important

24

is being able to return to your reflections later on. At this point you may recognize some themes emerging surrounding your experiences.

We are not our Stories

Meditation practices like this help us deal with difficult emotions as we can step into an awareness which goes beyond our ego and a fixed identity. From this awareness, where we are watching our mind, we develop the capacity to observe our emotions and experiences without becoming consumed by them. We realize that we are not the beliefs, thoughts or stories that are generated by our mind. These stories often comprise of our limiting beliefs – the ones that hold us back and tell us 'I'm not strong enough' or 'I can't deal with this'. They are the stories of who we think we are and how things should be. If we believe these stories are our reality then this can lead us to feel disempowered, stuck and unable to move forward. These stories can also create resistance towards our circumstances because we can get caught up in a fantasy of how things *should* or *could* be.

In the following section 'what are my beliefs' we will take a closer look at how to 're-write' these stories by focusing on our beliefs. We will identify what our current beliefs are in relation to the crisis and the losses we have experienced. Then, we'll have a go at constructing alternative beliefs to help us feel more empowered and resilient at this time.

I have found the following two activities, for addressing our beliefs and connecting with our core self, to be really helpful ways to let go of the stories of who we were in the past – (which we often get stuck in) and connecting with a more authentic, empowered, core self which can provide us with the resilience and strength we need during challenging times.

What are my beliefs?

Take a moment now to recognize what beliefs you are holding

onto in regards to your emotions and the experience you are going through right now. Have a go at completing the following sentences:

- I believe that grief is…
- I think that anger is…
- I think that I need to…
- If I were to feel all my sadness I would…
- Feeling lonely is…
- I believe I am….
- If I fully experience my despair I…

Consider which beliefs might be holding you back or limiting you from healing and navigating your emotions right now. What are some alternative beliefs, or stories you can write in relation to your emotions and the experiences you are going through? See if you can re-write these beliefs into positive affirmations or stories which will support you through your process (the following practice under 'Our Core Self' will be helpful for this).

It has been in the midst of some of my most challenging experiences that I've had the opportunity to recognize the stories I continued to tell myself. In the past, I have found myself lost in narratives that positioned myself in the role of a victim to the world around me, where I believed that something was being done to me and it was out of my control. When I learnt to become the observer of my thoughts, to watch the narrative surrounding my emotions, I was able to change those scripts into ones of empowerment and of choice, stories that enrich the capability to strive amid adversity. How do we do this? The ability to do this stems from the energetic center that rests in our solar plexus and which is always present with us. It is a strong, centered, courageous energy that is our core, most resilient self.

Our Core Self

Generating more courage, strength and resilience to navigate profound loss and grief can be achieved by connecting with our core self. This is the self that is stable, centered and eternal. This self is separate from the ego or the mind which holds onto limiting beliefs and can be more critical – telling us we're not good enough and caught up in strong emotions like fear or anxiety.

We can connect with this core self through the energetic center found in and around our navel. You may want to visualize or imagine this core self like an internal sun as it is also connected to the element of fire. It is a glowing sphere of vibrant light that is always present. Even when it feels like we have shifted into the shadow and we can no longer feel the warmth of its energy – the sun is still there and always emanating this powerful light.

So, this core self can also be understood as the seat of our consciousness or the one that witnesses our mind without being overwhelmed by it. After we've been through significant loss and transition, we may feel disempowered and overwhelmed by doubts and fears. There is a sense that we are no longer in control of our lives. This is a normal reaction to loss and momentous change, yet, it usually stems from the stories we have mentioned above, and an overactive mind which is searching for certainty and a way to survive the stress we are going through. So, as we go through the periods of chaos and challenge, it is helpful to connect with the energy center of our core self, which enables us to feel empowered to take positive action. To do this, we must connect with this part of us in a loving way – not forcing this connection but allowing this energy to arise form a place of authenticity. The following exercise is helpful for cultivating energy in this part of us. The activity is also a follow on from 'what are our beliefs' enabling us to construct alternative statements in relation to our ability to stay strong, resilient and centered in times of crisis.

Practice: Connecting with our Core Self

Close your eyes or leave them open and settle into your body. Bring awareness to your breath and to any physical sensations that are present. Rest and settle your body into the chair and feel grounded. Notice what's around you, the temperature of the room, sounds or smells and settle into an acceptance for everything that is in your awareness - don't try to change anything.

Now, shift awareness to the area of your stomach, just above your navel. You can even place your hand here if you'd like. You're going to take 5 deep breaths, breath in deeply through the nose and imagine your belly is a balloon expanding as much as possible, and then filling your chest with air (it's a circular breath) and then, without forcing the air out, let the belly deflate naturally. You're going to repeat this 5 times, and each time you breathe into the belly I want you to imagine you are filling it with vital energy and bringing this part of your body to life. You are restoring and nourishing it and letting go of stagnant, heavy or unnecessary energy. How does this part of your body feel? What is present for you right now? Is it soft, tense? Is it heavy or light? What does it need?

Visualize a yellow light here, a light which is warm, glowing like a bright sun. This is the light of your own self-motivation, your will, your courage and your strength. This light reflects a centered, strong and resilient self and remember - it is always present.

This light expands slowly, growing until it surrounds you as a field of strength. Feel your courage and resilience growing with it and your ability to stay strong and protected amidst the challenges around you.

Think of a time you have felt this connection, vitality and strength in the past and where this power flowed through you like warmth from the sun. Feel your body radiate with this energy.

What was this time, and how did it support you? What did it enable you to overcome? Feel that energy and visualize how you are present in the world when you are guided by this energy. How do you stand? How do you speak to others? How do take care of yourself? What actions are you taking?

Now bring to mind, something you are needing some courage, will or strength with right now. I want you to connect with the felt sense of the energy in your abdomen and you're going to complete the phrases:

"I can"... so it might be, 'I can get through these difficulties right now'
"I have the will..."
"I have the strength to deal with uncertainty right now"
"I am..."
"I am strong"
"I am resilient"
"I am courageous"
"I am directed by my intuition"

Now, visualize yourself making choices and taking action from this centered, empowered part of you. Remember you are also guided by your intuition. What does your intuition tell you? What do you see yourself doing as you move forward? How much are these actions aligned with your core values and your sacred self?

Now, as we bring this meditation to a close, allow the light, the heat and the size of this energy we have been visualizing, to settle into a steady, constant, burning flame, like a candle which is just the right size and intensity for you to go about your day-to-day activities, neither too strong not too weak. Allow it to stay constant and know that this light is always there, it is always within you – you can connect with it anytime you need its strength and courage.

Six Steps to Navigate Difficult Emotions

As we have said, one of the essential elements when navigating the journey of loss and grief is to open the door, wholeheartedly, to all our emotions. If we try to resist anger, fear or any other 'negative emotions' they will undoubtedly grow stronger and manifest in our bodies in other ways. This following practice is helpful for creating space and allowing all your experiences to be there, fully as they are. A practice such as this, also enables us to activate the parasympathetic nervous system and reduce the sympathetic nervous system.

Sympathetic and Parasympathetic Nervous System

The sympathetic nervous system is the fight, flight or freeze response and it is a natural response to perceived threat or danger. It is activated to keep us safe and protect us from any harm. When we experience loss and instability in our lives, we may enter a flight, flight or freeze response because our sense of safety has been compromised. This all serves a purpose when we must protect ourselves from danger, yet the body cannot identify the difference between serious life-threatening situations or a potential threat to our safety. Therefore, if this system is activated for too long it can have a detrimental effect on our body which includes a less effective immune system; trouble sleeping, tension in the body, physical pain and outbursts of strong emotion.

It is important to engage in practices that help lessen the time that the sympathetic nervous system is triggered and instead, start the "rest and digest system" (the parasympathetic nervous system). This system conserves energy, relaxes the body, slows the heart rate and promotes healing. Our ability to slip into this state is crucial during a crisis so that we can take time to heal our mind and body and handle our emotions more readily. When we're in a more relaxed state we're able to make decisions from a balanced perspective and we are also more likely to reach out to others for connection – this reaching out for connection is crucial when we're feeling isolated or alone. It also improves the functioning of our immune system, and if our body wasn't able to rest in this way, we would end up reaching a point of mental exhaustion and start to suffer from more serious mental or physical health issues.

One way to activate this part of the nervous system is to

engage in mindfulness practices such as the one suggested here. Go through these six steps: notice, breathe, expand, rest in the space, offer self-compassion and open awareness around your experience.

Notice

Notice what feelings or sensations are present in the body. Scan your body all the way from the top to the bottom and be curious as to what is showing up without placing any judgmental onto your experience. Remember that you are watching your experience and that this feeling, sensation or emotion is not the whole of you – it is a part of you that is here for a reason, and you are simply noticing its presence in you.

Breathe

As you're observing these feelings and sensations, breathe into them. Imagine your breath flowing into and around the sensations and this releases any tension or resistance you might have towards the sensations. The breath is always present, so you can always use it to relax into the experience you're having, and this will help prepare you for the following stages.

Expand

As you breathe into the sensations allow space to open up around these feelings. You are making space for the sensation to be present and with each breath you might visualize more space being created – allowing more room for your emotions to breathe. Perhaps the feelings are contracting and expanding with the movement of your breath or are pulsing and softening even more with the breathing and expansion that is taking place.

Rest in the space

Now, as you continue to breathe into these sensations, see if you can allow the feelings to be there. You are letting them know they are welcome and there is nothing you need to change, fix or get rid of. It is a complete acceptance of the feeling, sensation and emotions that are present for you.

Self-compassion

Take one of your hands and place it on the part of your body where you are feeling the sensation the most. You are going to imagine that this hand is sending healing energy to this area. You are offering it complete acceptance and loving compassion. You accept whatever is there, regardless of the quality of the sensation, or whether you want to label it as good or bad. Hold your hand on this part of your body for as long as is needed and allow the compassionate energy to flow into it. Continue to breathe into your experience and notice what happens as you do this.

Open awareness

Now, allow your awareness to expand outwards encompassing your whole body, so you can now feel all parts and all sensation. You will notice the movement of breath and energy flowing to the different areas of your body. We will take this even further and now become aware of what is going on outside and around you – so this involves awareness of your external space. What sights, sound and smells are you aware of. Where is your body in relation to your environment? What perspective do you gain from moving your awareness outwards in this way? Now, see if you can hold this space in your awareness, while simultaneously staying connected to your body and the sensations we have focused on.

When you have worked through the six steps, take a moment to recognize what is present for you. Did this practice soften any resistance to feelings of anger or sadness? Do these emotions feel more welcomed into you? What is your mind telling you about your emotions – notice what thoughts, stories and beliefs are coming up for you? It is always a good idea to write these down so you can keep a record of your experiences.

Disowned Emotions and the Shadow

The earlier exercises are vitally important so that we don't disown the difficult emotions that arise through times of loss and grief. Unfortunately, society has often led us to feel ashamed or want to hide our emotions. When we grieve for the things that we have lost, it is common to hear phrases like 'don't worry,' 'be strong,' or 'there are people worse off'. It is crucial we do not negate the relevance of our emotions like this, otherwise, they become disowned parts of ourselves which then enter into our shadow.

Carl Jung first referred to the shadow as the part of ourselves that we have rejected, disowned or denied. We may not even know that certain emotions or behaviors exist, or have the potential to exist within us, because they are so deeply repressed within us. When we inhibit our emotions in this way, we project them onto others and the world around us. These qualities become external things we either judge, feel frightened of or are irritated by.

Even when we are not fully aware of our shadow, its presence uses a vast amount of energy which can cause physical, mental and emotional exhaustion. We use this energy to portray a particular image of ourselves to the world and it's like constantly putting on a mask of how we want others or the outside world to perceive us. This might be by trying to show others we are strong, resilient and brave. Yet, as I mentioned before, cultivating resilience through the path of loss and uncertainty is actually about being vulnerable enough to embrace the emotions and the struggle that we are encountering. As times of crisis continue to unfold, we are called to bring our shadow into our awareness and to embrace the totality of our human experience. When we are 'broken open' through the space of loss and grief then the darker emotions that we want to deny are brought to the surface. If we avoid this process and continue to put on a mask, not allowing ourselves to be vulnerable enough to share our emotions of sadness and grief then these emotions will continue to lie underneath the mask, often growing in intensity and then get projected onto others or the outside. We become defensive and this mask may turn into a wall of protection, stopping us from opening our hearts fully. When I am struggling with powerful emotions such as sadness, or anger, which tend to show up regularly in the process of loss and grief, I have found that engaging in a creative exercise to express those emotions is helpful.

Activities

- Create a piece of art or a drawing from the angle of an emotion that you are finding it difficult to express. This might be a drawing from the perspective of sadness, anger or loneliness.
- Write a poem or a creative piece of writing from the point of view of the emotion. This could be an "I am" poem. What does that emotion see, feel, hear? What does the emotion want to express to you? What needs to be known or revealed about its experience? What does it want to share with the world? Why is it showing up in the way it is? How is it trying to help you? These questions are helpful to ask, as you take on the mindset of this emotion.
- Write a letter from the viewpoint of the emotion to yourself, or from yourself to your emotion welcoming it into you. This helps to bring the emotion closer to you and to counteract any parts of you that may want to deny or push this emotion away. If you are writing a letter to the emotion itself, write it from a compassionate space, welcoming it and letting it know that it has a right to be there. Speak to it, just as you would speak to a small, innocent child. If you write the letter from the perspective of the emotion you are allowing the relationship between that emotion and your true self to be strengthened,

creating a healthy and open communication between the various parts of yourself.

- Dance the emotion or act it out. Embody it and step into its energy. If the emotion was an animal or a specific movement, what would it be? Does it take on the energy of any elements, could it be the flow of water? Does it take on the vibrancy of a raging fire? How do you embody this energy and allow it to be expressed healthily, so that the energy can move freely through you? I find this exercise is helpful for those who are more tactile or experience the world kinesthetically through the felt sense of the body. This also, allows us to connect more deeply with the emotions and what is going on intuitively in the body and not just the intellectual or rational mind alone.

This chapter has shared the importance of fully embracing all our emotions from a space of vulnerability, openness and acceptance. We spoke about the shadow, and I feel this is a crucial element of going through an individual or collective crisis. It can be compared to a glass of water that is holding deposits of sand at the bottom. The sand is our collective shadow; the glass has been shaken and the grains of sand stirred into our awareness. This can cause a great deal of suffering, chaos and disharmony as we embrace the emotions and realities that we don't necessarily want to look at. Yet, it is unhealthy to let the sand continue to rest in the glass's bottom for too long – it needs to be brought into conscious awareness, so we can begin to transform and heal it. In times of crisis, we have an opportunity to embrace and heal our individual and collective suffering and the best way to do this is through the practice of compassion, beginning first with acts of self-compassion.

Chapter 4

Compassion

"Your fundamental nature is pure, conscious, peaceful, radiant, loving and wise and it is joined in mysterious ways with the ultimate underpinnings of reality"
Rick Hanson

Welcoming our Emotions with Compassion

We have spoken about how helpful it is to use mindfulness techniques to connect with the felt sense of the emotions in our body and become the observer of our minds. We can take it a step further by not only bringing awareness and space to our emotions but welcoming them into us wholeheartedly and with compassion.

Compassion literally means to 'suffer together'. Before we can have true compassion for others, we need to foster compassion for ourselves and be willing to reduce our suffering through conscious practices. This means to welcome our pain rather than ignore it, to remember that we do not suffer alone because experiences of loss, endings and grief are shared by all of us. This doesn't mean we take on the suffering of the world or become a victim to it, but it reminds us that 'we're all in this together'.

One of the reasons I find self-compassionate exercises so helpful is because we're not trying to achieve anything through the process. The goal isn't to feel better, or to get rid of anything. Actually, there is no goal! It is simply about recognizing what is present and holding space for it, like you would embrace a small, vulnerable child. When we see a small baby crying in front of us, it is our instinct to pick the baby up – to hold and nurture them. We also need to do that for ourselves and our emotions. When we are suffering from loss, we feel particularly vulnerable and fragile and the wounds we have are raw – so we must learn to take care of them.

When we are navigating the unknown it feels like we are floating in an expansive space with no solid ground below us. There is an urgency to move forward or find some stability again. Of course, we all want this and many of us wish things were as they were before our crisis came along. Some of us might start to daydream about how life is going to be when this is over. Yet, there is something particularly important about staying present with what is right now – whether we feel loss or hope, sadness or gratitude, fear or love, no matter the experience we need to hold space for it, for us and for each other.

Cultivating compassion is an essential practice when navigating periods of loss and grief. It is shown that those who are more self-compassionate tend to be less anxious, stressed and depressed. It also helps us to connect more deeply with others – being more open to connection and communication, which is essential during these times. Some other benefits of self-compassion include bringing greater equanimity to our experience. This means that our experiences are neither suppressed nor exaggerated. We stay mindful and observe our experiences just as they are.

Everyone deserves self-compassion, we are not compassionate based on how good or bad we are as a person, but we offer compassion because we are living beings and we are all worthy of being held in a safe, protective and loving way. Sometimes we can fall into the trap of believing that our suffering is not worthy of attention, we might think 'others are suffering more, others have more pain that I do' or 'I *should* be grateful'. It is true that there are millions of people in the world who are going through excruciating difficulties and the chances are, we *do* have a lot to be grateful for (we will talk about gratitude in the next chapter) but if we only focus on gratitude there is a danger of by-passing the difficulties that we need to go through first.

Self-Compassion Meditation

Settle into your body by taking a few deep breaths. Inhale through your nose and out through your mouth. And again in through your nose and out through your mouth. Take one last deep breath in through your nose and out through your mouth. Take a few minutes to recognize what physical sensations are present in your body. Start with your toes, feet, lower legs, knees, upper legs, buttocks, hips, lower back, middle back, upper back, shoulders, back of your neck, head, forehead, eyes, nose, mouth, throat area, down to your chest, heart, stomach. You might be able to label certain sensations. Now, breathe into them.

Next, ask yourself, "What is happening inside me right now?" Notice what stories are present, what thoughts and beliefs are your mind telling you right now about your experience? What is it telling you about what is going on in the world or about who you are as a person?

Now see if there is a judgement, or a desire to change your experience. Or, are you able to let it all be there simply as it is? See if you can use your in and out breath to surrender to what is here without trying to push anything away or change it. Notice how it feels to drop into the experience, to let it be and to allow it. Sit with that feeling for a moment.

When we allow all parts of ourselves to be present we embrace the dark and the light, we hold love and fear together and know that all these emotions, all aspects, all parts contribute towards our reality and have a right to be here.

Next, we will continue to bring a kind and compassionate awareness to our experience. See if you can notice what is calling for your attention the most, see if you can go further into your experience and be curious about it. Communicate with what is present, ask what is calling for your attention, ask what is needed? What wants to be seen or to be known? See what arises and notice if the sensations, thoughts or feelings shift as you explore everything with an attitude of non-judgmental openness. You might even notice a space emerge between your thoughts, between the emotions and sensations like there is an expansion taking place.

We are now going to open our hearts even more fully to offer compassion and send warmth and loving energy to whatever is present for us right now. If it feels difficult to offer yourself this compassion, bring to mind a loving being – a spiritual figure, a family member, a friend or an element of nature and imagine that being's love and wisdom flowing into you. If there is a particular sensation in your body that is calling for your attention you might place your hand on this part of your body now. Imagine enfolding it in a heart of compassion, a heart of warm loving, healing energy. Tell yourself, 'I accept all that is present in me right now', if there are any difficult emotions present tell yourself, 'I welcome all that is difficult'. Allow your heart to soften in this process. Say thank you to those experiences, emotions, and feelings that are present in you.

Now, when you are ready take a deep breath in through your nose and out through your mouth, gently opening your eyes if they have been closed and just notice what is present for you in this moment.

Know your Needs

Self-compassion is also about respecting our needs so that we can find ways to nurture these. This is especially important when we have experienced profound loss. Our needs may fall into the following areas: mental, emotional, physical, spiritual and interpersonal needs. During times of loss and grief, we feel emotionally and physically vulnerable and we may not be able to receive care and support from others in the way that we are used to. It is easy to neglect or even feel guilty for wanting to take care of ourselves; we might feel that it is not important right now because there are other more pressing issues to take care of. We must find ways to offer this care and compassion to ourselves because it is these acts of self-care and respect that will help us to heal and navigate our difficult circumstances more graciously.

The more you engage in small, nourishing acts of self-care such as: taking a bath; going for a walk in nature; getting enough restful sleep or choosing healthy food – the more ability you will have to stay present with your grief and difficult emotions at this time. Take a moment to consider what your mental, emotional, spiritual, interpersonal and physical needs are. What does it feel is lacking in your life right now? What do you need more of? Is it more rest, time to reflect or do you need more space than usual? Are you searching for ways to feel connected spiritually, to engage in rituals, meditation or time to journal about your experiences? Do you need more physical affection or touch? Does finding time for fun or playful activities feel important to you right now? Whatever your needs are, know that they are worthy of being attended to. Here are some suggestions for how to address some of our needs during this time:

- Write a journal to keep a record of your emotions. This might be something you do first thing in the morning, or before you go to sleep at night. Take 15 minutes to write down everything that has arisen for you, in the form of a steady flow of consciousness. This activity is helpful for expressing any emotions you are experiencing and allowing them to be acknowledged.

- Make an arrangement with some close friends where you are checking in on each other regularly. This might include something as small as a text message each day, or a weekly phone call. Letting your friends and family know that you are there to listen to each other is really important for creating a sense of community when things are difficult.

- Set up or take part in a weekly meeting with a group of friends or a small community of people online. Knowing that you have a regular meeting, with the same group of people each week, is something to really look forward to and will help fulfil your need for connection and community.

- No matter what your spiritual or religious beliefs are, you may want to set up a specific place in your house where you can engage in your spiritual practice. This might be as simple as having a photograph or a statue of a spiritual figure of a loved one, some flowers or a meditation cushion which you know is always available to you. It is also helpful to have this sacred place in your home to connect with loved ones who have passed away and take the time to remember them.

- If you are struggling from a lack of physical touch or connection with others, find a way to connect with nature. When you go for walks, really feel into the ground below you – even dig your hands into the soil or the grass. Lean against a tree, take a moment to observe the color of the sky. Look around you, what are five things you can really notice in your surroundings? (I recommend *Connecting with Nature in a Time of Crisis*, by Melanie Choukas-Bradley, which is also part of the Resilience Series).

- When taking part in other activities like having a bath, turn it into a ritual process. Light candles, play music, burn incense and make it an active process rather than a passive activity.

- Create a timetable or a routine which helps form some structure around your day. This can be as simple as a list of activities you want to try and accomplish each day or something more structured with set times for certain practices. This is especially helpful if you are working from home and have a more flexible routine that you are used to.

- Physical activity and exercise is really crucial. If you are spending a lot of time sitting, or your energy is feeling quite stagnant, try and take some time to practice yoga, go for a run, follow an online fitness routine or join one of the many online classes that are being offered. This is not only good for your physical health, but it will help to lift your mood and release anxiety, anger or other strong emotions.

- This can be a good time to learn something new, take an online course or engage in a hobby that you have always wanted to – but perhaps haven't had time for in the past. What is something you would like to learn? Is there a goal you can now start working towards?

Letting Go

"Letting go is like the sudden cessation of an inner pressure or the dropping of a weight. It is accompanied by a sudden feeling of relief and lightness, with an increased happiness and freedom"
Dr. David R Hawkins

When life takes us in a direction we had not planned for, where the dreams we had and the goals we were working towards are left unfulfilled, it is normal for us to experience disappointment, frustration, anger or resentment. When we hold onto the idea of how things were supposed to be or should have been it only creates tension and a stickiness, which then creates even more suffering in us. This relates to the stages of anger or bargaining that we spoke about when working through grief.

Letting go of the need to control the outcome, or the struggle we feel when things don't go as planned, is about accepting and dropping into the space of loss and uncertainty that we are experiencing. Letting go of emotions like fear, anger or frustration doesn't mean to reject or deny them as it is not the same as aversion or struggling to get rid of something. We cannot genuinely let go of what we resist as it will only come back stronger and with more vengeance. To let go means to feel everything fully and accept it all just as it is.

When we hold our emotions close to us, we also surrender to

our vulnerability and step into a space of humility. When we say 'I see you, I am here' we rest in the space of stillness and are able to let go. We let go of parts of us that have been wanting to hold onto a particular way of being, we let go of the ego which had an alternative plan for us or thought it was able to control how our lives were going to be.

It is difficult to let go of what is so familiar to us. We might be afraid – and you might ask yourself "who will I be if I let go of these ways of being?' However, the identity and roles we present to the world are just parts of us – they are not our core self. When we experience loss, and we let go, there is often an unraveling of the many layers of our ego with enables our core, authentic self to shine through.

When I left Shanghai I travelled and worked, for almost a year, in different parts of the world before settling in London. During this time, I experienced an unraveling of my 'fixed identity'. I let go of many roles and labels that I was ascribed to through my work, my friendship group and as a result of the different activities I was involved in. I also let go of an attachment to material possessions because I either left these behind or put them in storage. When I introduced myself to new people, I found myself sharing who I was rather than what I *did*. I didn't necessarily need or want to 'get rid of' these roles and the process was difficult but transformative. This is probably the case for many people who experience sudden and unexpected losses in times of crisis. There is something liberating and deeply healing in the freedom that comes when we become less attached to what we thought was 'fixed'. When we let go, in this way, we have a chance to connect with the depth of who we really are and choose how we want to move forward with our lives. So, although a time of transition may be difficult, it's truly a gift to be able to operate from a more authentic place; we let go of our conditioned self but not our core self.

Letting Go Rituals

Rituals can be a powerful way of letting go of the things which don't serve us anymore. They help us to shift beliefs and enable us to connect and align with a sacred energy that is much greater than our individual selves. They are, therefore, powerful and effective at releasing old patterns and stagnant energy. The following exercise focusses on letting go of the things that might be causing us to resist our circumstances or how things have turned out because of the crisis we are in.

Questions

- What am I ready or willing to let go of today?
- Is it an emotion that is no longer serving you or a limiting belief about yourself and your situation?
- Is it time to let this emotion or feelings go?
- Is holding onto this emotion helping me?

Allow the answers to these questions to arise from the space of your heart. In this ritual process it is important to connect with the energetic, felt sense of letting go. So become aware of how these beliefs or emotions resonate in your body. Once you have written everything down, set the intention to let them go and take part in a ritual process that is symbolic for you. The following visualization is a helpful guide and you can also adapt it or incorporate it into your own ritual or routine.

Letting Go Exercise

First, take a few deep breaths and settle into your body as we have done in the previous exercises. Use the breath to settle your body and let go of any tension you might be holding onto. Feel the benefit that will come from this ritual of letting go.

Say to yourself, 'I let go', 'I release you'. And allow this process to occur as much as it is possible – you don't need to force anything. Soften the body, the heart and mind and now visualize how the beliefs or emotions you're letting go of are filtering out of you into the earth. Notice how the feelings are released like water flowing out of a cup and the energy of them is also transformed as they are released. Recognize the space that arrives as you begin this processing of letting go, notice how the heart softens and the body expands.

Now take one last deep breath in and out, and when you are ready open your eyes. What has shifted as you released the energy of those emotions and beliefs? What has been freed up in the process? How does your body and mind feel now? Stay with this energy and breathe into the changes that take place. What can now manifest in the space that has been created?

Some alternatives to the visualization above include:

- Write down everything that you feel ready to let go of. Now, as you feel the sense of letting it all go, tear up the paper that you've written on or even put it in a shredder! As you tear the paper up, or watch the shredding process, really step into the energy of releasing these old beliefs. If you have a small, safe fireplace you can throw the papers into the fire. If you're outside, you can watch them be carried away by the wind. Performing this ritual in an open space like your garden or a park can be a powerful process.
- Water is a powerful element which carries strong emotions. Take an object like a leaf or a stick – something which will stay afloat in water. You're going to use the object to represent what it is you would like to let go of. Place the object in a river, stream or a small body of water. Now, allow the object to be carried away. Watch it drift away and in the process connect with the felt sense that comes with being able to release what you no longer need to hold onto. If you don't have access to a stream or river near your house, you can simply visualize this activity.

Once we set an intention to let go and engage in a ritual for doing so, there is an energetic shift that takes place; we've freed up mental, emotional and spiritual energy which allows us to bring new energy into our lives. You will see fresh opportunities, people and relationships appear and you'll generally feel lighter and more at ease. Now, all there is to do, is stay present with the extra space that has been created and rest in a space of surrender.

Resting in a space of surrender gives us the opportunity to reach into parts of our soul that we have, at some point, lost connection with. It is a sinking into uncertainty, falling through an open space and not knowing where we will land. It is about trusting in the process and knowing that wherever we fall will be the right place. It has been in these moments of surrender where I have connected with the knowing that we are part of a collective intelligence and an ocean of consciousness which is always working towards harmony. Our ability to drop into this space also means we can enter a state of flow. In the following section I will explore in more detail, the concept of entering flow, the relationship between resilience and being vs doing, grounding ourselves and finding that 'place where we land'.

Entering Flow

Entering a space of acceptance frees up a lot of energy in our body and mind. We move from a place of stickiness, resistance, hesitation and feeling frozen, into a space of expansion and movement; an ability to flow freely. Letting go and entering this state of flow is not something we can force; it is a natural process that we can only embrace and step into when the time is right. We can compare it to a leaf, floating effortlessly down a stream. The leaf does not need to control the process or try to direct its course, but it is carried freely by the current which takes it exactly where it needs to go. This state of flow is something we can embrace within our own lives and the following practice will help us to stay connected to the energy of flow.

Meditation for Expansion & Flow

Close your eyes and step into a sense of freedom and ease as you accept your emotions and your situation just as they are. Connect with the vibrational energies of love, peace, happiness and acceptance. How does it feel to live each moment deeply connected to the energy of openness and flow? Welcome this creative force into you and notice where and how that energy moves in your body. You might sense it flowing freely like water or acknowledge it as an expansion. A specific image may come to mind, if so, just watch it. Do you feel lighter? Is there a felt sense of connecting with something beyond your body? Breathe into that energy and the expansive, open space – what do you see? What do you feel? Stay connected to your senses. And while in this state of flow, ask yourself: what is something I can do to stay connected with this energy in the following hours, days, or weeks to come? See what appears here and set the intention to stay present with this energy as much as possible in the following days. Continue to repeat this practice as much as you feel is necessary. You might even choose to take 5 minutes every morning to enter into this state of flow and thus, enable you to carry out your day-to-day activities with more peace and acceptance.

Balancing Being vs Doing

Entering 'lock-down' has been a gradual transition from a state of 'over-doing' into a space of *being* present with what is. Many of us have been conditioned into always needing to be productive; to achieve a specific task; complete a set goal or use our time in the most valuable way. There might be an urgency to find solutions to our losses, to keep busy and find ways to distract ourselves from our suffering. Taking action is important, yet the energy of 'over-doing' is a side-effect of a heavily goal driven society which demands we keep going and striving all the time. According to Gareth Hill, a Jungian analyst, this is characteristic of the dynamic masculine and the willful goal directed. The masculine is an archetypal force, not a gender and we are offered the opportunity during times of crisis to move closer towards, what Gareth Hill called the static feminine, to allow for more balance and enter a more natural, organic flow.

Often the energy behind 'over-doing' can be fueled by fear and uncertainty about our future as we have a natural desire to seek out certainty and find solutions. Yet, the feminine energy teaches us to stop, rest and pay attention to what is present without a specific goal or outcome in mind. How much time do you allow yourself to be present with no kind of goal, expectation or desired outcome? As we take this time to slow down, can we alternate between the desire to take action, then the need to stop and rest? Can we find an equilibrium between the two?

Striking this balance between the masculine and feminine energies feels crucial and it's also highly related to the act of self-compassion. Our acceptance of the *is,* and our ability to give space in our life for rest and relaxation has been neglected by so many of us, in our fast paced, materialistic, goal driven society. *Being* doesn't mean you're a passive recipient towards your situation, and as we speak about in this book, we can still consciously choose practices to support us through our journey, while at the same time, acknowledge that we can breathe and surrender into a space of acceptance for the reality of our circumstances.

Chapter 5

Grounding

Grounding Ourselves

As we traverse these turbulent times, many of us will feel a lack of community, a lack of connection, and a lack of belonging. When we experience loss, a feeling of security and safety is also abruptly taken from us. An awareness of chaos, uncertainty and the instability of life is brought directly into our consciousness. This is why it's so important to find an alternative way to ground ourselves – especially when powerful emotions are coming to the surface.

We can draw on the Eastern knowledge of the chakras, and in particular the root chakra, as a way to develop greater stability and a sense of grounding in our body. The chakras are energy centers located in different parts of our body and the root chakra, located at the base of the spine, acts like an anchor to help us feel more supported. If this energy center is depleted or we perceive ourselves as being separate from the collective ecosystem that we are a part of, then we are less likely to remain steady and resilient during times of adversity. So, just like a tree which has strong, firm roots, it is necessary to have a solid foundation for us to build everything else upon.

Meditation: Grounding and Connecting

We're going to use the following visualization to balance our root chakra and re-establish a connection with the earth. We will bring the energy from the earth in our bodies, to nourish us and remind ourselves that we are part of something much greater than our individual ego. We will also send energy back outwards and empower ourselves into the knowing that we also contribute to a collective, shared energy. Then, we will work to connect with the energies of each other, so even though we may be far apart from each other while we are in lockdown: in separate rooms, separate spaces, or houses we are still connected and part of a network, a community and a collective field of consciousness.

Take a moment to settle into your body either sitting or lying down. Make sure you are comfortable and lay a blanket over you if needed. Take a few strong breaths, inhaling deeply through your nose and out through your mouth. With each breath, allow yourself to surrender, let go and relax completely.

Either with your eyes open or closed, bring your attention to the base of your spine, to the area of your root chakra and see if you can visualize it at the back of your body, where your tailbone is touching the chair, or the bed – if you are laying down.

Now visualize a red ball of light at this area, which is glowing brightly and expanding here. Continue to observe this image for a minute, noticing how brightly it is shining, imagine it is swirling in a clockwise direction, a red ball of light rotating clockwise. And it might increase or decrease in size. Just allow it to be there and notice it; feel the energy of it.

Now from this ball of light, I want you to visualize roots emerging and growing from it. Notice their color, texture, length, size and the density of these roots. When the image is clear in your mind, become aware of how these roots are growing longer and longer. Visualize them moving down, through the ground, into the soil and the earth below. Perhaps moving through your legs and feet. Notice how these roots create a strong energetic connection with the earth and realize how you are being fully supported and held by the physical ground below you.

Now, there is a white, bright energy coming from the ground - where these roots have planted themselves. Notice this energy and its quality. It is a nourishing, strong and vibrant energy. Recognize how there is an exchange of energy that is taking place between your body and the earth, via these roots. There is energy moving downwards, and energy coming from the earth itself. As this flow of energy continues notice how you are bringing more and more health, strength and stability into your body. Allow yourself to receive what you need to receive through this flow of energy. What are you able to give? What balances this exchange of energy and keeps it equal?

In your own mind, repeat the following affirmations to yourself, "I am here. I am supported, I am safe, I am grounded".

Now we will take a moment to feel a sense of grounding and of being rooted to the earth. With this solid foundation I want you to imagine this energy that we have cultivated here, moving upwards throughout the rest of your body. Imagine that energy seeping into each and every cell of your body and nourishing you. As we do this, imagine that this energy is not limited to the cells of your body, but it is reaching out to others, connecting with the whole of humanity. It is a pure, nourishing, wholesome and healing energy. Recognize our interdependence and allow this energy to go beyond our connection with each other to encompass a greater whole. You can visualize this in any way you want, there is no right or wrong – allow whatever images arise that need to emerge.

Then, take a moment to repeat the following statements:

- *I am a part of a collective, a whole, a greater consciousness*
- *I am being held and I trust that I am supported and safe*
- *I am connected to everything that is in my awareness*

Now, while keeping that connection to others and to the greater whole, allow yourself to come back to your body – to the here and now. Feel the connection of your body on the floor, bed or chair. Take a few deep breaths, scanning your body for any shifts or sensations that are present. Slowly, in your own time, if your eyes have been closed, open them back up again.

Chapter 6

Finding Perspective

"It's not impermanence that makes us suffer. What makes us suffer is wanting things to be permanent when they are not" Thich Nhat Hanh

Acceptance of Impermanence

We know that everything in life must at some point come to an end and all things are moving through a constant cycle of change. Yet, it is still very normal to become attached to the people, places and things we love – thinking they are going to be this way forever. It is also natural to want to hold on to our material possessions and what we have worked hard for over the years. It is healthy to form attachments to family, friends and to desire loving relationships. These attachments and desires are what make endings so difficult, especially when they happen very suddenly and unexpectedly. This concept of change and the impermanence of all things, reminds us to appreciate each and every moment of our lives and to generate gratitude. Directly experiencing loss and the experience of grief that comes with loss begins to shift our perspective in this way.

When I resist the process of letting go and I'm attached to an outcome of how things *should* be, or when I try to control a process, I find myself struggling with strong emotions such as anger, frustration, irritation and anxiety. When the COVID-19 crisis hit, I fell into resistance because of the abrupt nature of my losses. Yet, I could never have imagined what would emerge from the space that I entered, when I surrendered to these endings! I remember all the moments in my life, where the most painful of endings became the catalysts for significant periods of transition and growth.

Recently, during a lucid dream, I received an image which continued to play on repeat in my mind. It was an image of a forest moving through the cycles of life and death. I saw the flowers, trees and every living creature in the forest wallow and fall into ashes and decay; darkness arrived and the forest turned to grey dust. From the ashes and the desolate, barren dried up soil, a sprout emerged, a flower unfurled, color returned and the forest sprang to life again, into all its vibrancy, vitality, flow and movement. This cycle of life and death repeated itself in my mind during the dream and it reminded me of the inherent nature of our existence and how important is it for us to embrace the phases of life and death, as both are as valid and crucial to live our lives fully. I was also reminded of polarity, of lightness and darkness, and that it is necessary to embrace everything in its totality. It can be difficult to step into the darkness, the decay and the dust – it takes courage to do so, yet, when we do this, we also enter into new beginnings.

Finding Meaning and Purpose

It is through times of extreme adversity that we are called to re-evaluate what is important to us. A loss of any kind can strip us of the very things which gave us purpose, whether it is our job, a relationship, an ability to connect with our loved ones, our identity or our sense of freedom. Yet, history shares with us the incredible resilience that is generated by people who find themselves in unexpected moments of crisis. These experiences of crisis not only highlight their innate strength and courage to get through challenging times, but their ability to discover meaning and purpose despite their adversity, and for some, find meaning because of their adversity.

I am reminded of the incredible story of my Grandfather, born in January 1921 in Ariano Irpino, a small village in South Italy. At the age of 18, on the onset of the Second World War, my grandfather was pulled away from his rural village and he began a life-changing journey which involved spending two-and-a-half years at Camp 60 as a prisoner of war on the island of Lamb Holm in the Orkney Islands just off Scotland. His legacy tells a story, not only of being a prisoner of war survivor, but of being part of a community who came together to find meaning and purpose within a time of struggle. During the two-and-a-half year stay my grandfather, who was an electrician, commenced a project with a group of men, to build a Chapel – a place of workshop to be used during their time as prisoners. As I researched my grandfather's story, I found the significance of them not only seeking a way to connect with their spiritual beliefs, but of them engaging in a project which formed community and gave them a joined purpose in their time of struggle.

Through my research, I found that the building of the Chapel, which my grandfather and the other men set out to accomplish, shifted something dramatic in their prison community – it removed the concept of "enemy" or "friend' and inspired a collective purpose shared by the prisoners, guards and other members of the camp. The relationships between the prisoners and guards continued to transform and a greater sense of community and shared purpose was built alongside the Chapel itself. I wonder if breaking down the notion of enemy or friend, building community and coming together as a collective, also plays an important role as we navigate our way through our current crisis. My grandad and his fellow prisoners had lost so much: their freedom, their homes, their families and their identity had been stripped. Yet, when they were able to construct something together it allowed them to connect with their spiritual beliefs and a sense of purpose was found – they found a way to move forward. I wonder how we as a global community can construct something meaningful together as we work through this crisis collectively, in support of each other.

The Chapel stands today as a lasting icon – one which preserves the story of my grandfather and the other prisoners of war. My grandfather's story reflects how we can transform hardship into hope, adversity into meaning and isolation into connection. This quote, from a fellow prisoner is written on a plaque on the entrance to the Chapel:

"It was the wish to show to oneself first, and to the world then, that in spite of being trapped in a barbed wire camp, down in spirit, physically and morally deprived of many things, one could still find something inside that could be set free."

The Inside of the Italian Chapel
Photo: Paul De Vitto

Spiritual Transformation

The word *spiritual* can be interpreted in many ways. From my perspective, spirituality is very distinct from religion and it is not about following a specific doctrine. It is about the awareness and connection to something greater than our individual self and this connection can be experienced in various forms. It might be through music, connection with nature, dance, rituals, healing work, yoga, meditation or engaging in an activity and entering a state of 'flow'. This makes spirituality a universal phenomenon and not specific to any particular culture, ethnicity or religion. When we have a direct experience of the 'spiritual' we are guided towards greater unity and connection with the whole and this brings greater healing, wholeness, meaning and purpose to our lives. So spirituality doesn't necessarily need to be taught, but it is something that is experienced and then understood universally.

It is my experience that loss, grief and periods of suffering is what often brings about this direct connection with our sacred self and our spiritual path. When I experience loss, I can also experience a breaking down of my ego, a dropping down of defenses and an ability to enter inter a space beyond my egoic self. When I have been overcome with the despair of losing a loved one, a relationship ending or feeling the loss of my dreams and joy, I have also experienced connecting to a more expansive reality. Loss and grief have become a bridge to my soul, a way to connect with truth, to open my heart to compassion and to live each day with gratitude. Without these experiences I don't think I would have been able to encounter the psychological and spiritual growth that I have. My experience is that as we are navigating the path of uncertainty, as many of us are at this time, we are given a choice: to give up entirely, to resist and try to fight it, or to surrender to an intelligence that goes beyond our individual selves. When a global pandemic moves throughout our lives in ways we are not prepared for, and impacting us in ways we cannot predict, we have the option to resist, give up or to connect more deeply with ourselves and with soul. As Viktor Frankl said,

"Everything can be taken from a person, but one thing: the last of the human freedoms - to choose one's attitude in any given set of circumstances, to choose one's own way"

We always have the choice to find meaning – no matter which situation, circumstance or space we find ourselves in. We do this by connecting to what is really important to us and then choosing to move forward based on our core values and what gives us purpose.

Depression

For some, the loss and grief that is experienced will catapult them into a period of depression. As we spoke about earlier, depression is one of the natural stages of grief and it is important for us to remember that depression is a normal response to loss. In fact, episodes of depression have the potential to trigger significant transformation in ourselves and offer a pathway to live a more authentic life.

The Dark Night of the Soul is known as a time of deep depression, or a spiritual crisis, where in the darkest moments of sorrow we might start asking what the purpose of our struggle is. We will confront many doubts and questions in relation to the meaning life. Yet, if we are prepared to find the strength and courage to move through the process and to navigate the challenges that have been presented to us, we will emerge on the other side, stronger and more resilient that we ever thought was possible. Carl Jung also speaks of the archetype of the wounded healer, based on the Greek myth of Chiron, where those who go through significant difficulties, or experiences of loss and grief may do so to heal and apply what they've learnt to help others. In Joseph Campbell's *The Hero's Journey* it is said that there is a point that takes us from safety into the unknown. We partake in a number of trials and tribulations and along the journey, there are setbacks and disappointments, yet, in the moments of despair where all hope appears to be lost, hidden parts of our soul will be brought to life, an inner strength is reached and an understanding of the purpose behind all our loss and struggles is revealed. (For more on depression, see the companion volume in this series: *Resilience: Handling Anxiety in a Time of Crisis*, by George Hofmann).

Values

Our values reflect the things which are meaningful to us in our lives, how we want to exist in the world and be remembered by others. Everyone's core values are different, for example, some of us place more importance on career over family, or relationships over finances. Our values can also change over time and as we move through life. It is my understanding that when navigating the difficulties of loss, we start to re-evaluate what is meaningful to us, and we connect with the values that stem from a more expansive and coherent self. We may begin to place more emphasis on things like family, relationships and loved ones over career and financial goals. The amount of emphasis that we place on the various domains of our life may begin to shift and when we come into a crisis, people's core values start to look remarkably similar. These are values of: love, connection, community, compassion and care.

The following activity will help you to connect with your core values. See what arises when you ask yourself the following:

Close your eyes and connect with the energy of your heart. Breathe into this area of your body and you might even place your hand here. Let the answers to the following questions come from your core self.

1. What really matters to you?
2. If you knew you only had a limited time left on this Earth, what do you want to do with your time? Who would you spend it with?
3. If you were able to look back on your life, what sort of person would you prefer to be remembered as? How would people describe your character? Are these the words you would like to hear about yourself?
4. What are the qualities you respect in other people? How could you strengthen those qualities in yourself?

Choose ten values that stand out to you and write the values down on post-it notes or slips of paper. The values might be things such as: communication, authenticity, connection. Place these words somewhere where you can see them regularly and continue to remind yourself of them. Each day when you see these words ask yourself:

1. Out of these ten values, which one's feel the most important to focus on today?
2. How much am I living in alignment with my values today?
3. What actions am I taking to move closer towards these values?

Once we are clear on our values, we are ready to live in alignment with these values and make choices or decisions based on these every day. It doesn't matter if we are in lockdown, or if we are isolated from our friends and family – we are still able to offer our compassion and support to others through social media and stay in virtual contact with them, thereby, we are still aligned with our value for connection and love. If honesty and respect are two of our core values, we can show these in small actions we take each day, such as how we choose to interact with our family members who we are in lockdown with, or when sat at our desks and making calls to work colleagues. We can also offer respect to our environment and to the world when we go out on our daily walks. There is always an opportunity to live in accordance to the things that are important in our life and to what gives us a greater sense of purpose. It is a good idea to keep a journal and make a note of the activities that you do each day when putting your values into action. This will bring a greater awareness to the actions you are taking, and this awareness will help to strengthen them.

Gratitude

Research has shown gratitude is a huge contributor towards resilience. It not only reduces stress, but it plays a major role in overcoming traumatic experiences. Connecting with all that you have to be thankful for, even during the worst times, will build resilience.

We may have taken many things for granted before we entered the pandemic: day-to-day interactions with others; our freedom to travel and see friends whenever we wanted; financial security and the wide variety of activities that are usually available to us. How often did we stop and offer appreciation for these things? Our routines become so familiar and we assume they will always be this way. It rarely occurs to us that the people and things we love could be taken away from us at any given moment and the reality of impermanence appears to be a central lesson during times of crisis. So, although there are many things missing from our lives right now – we still have so much to be grateful for. Taking part in conscious practices to generate gratitude for what is still present in our lives is a healthy way to feel stronger and more centered in times of crisis.

Gratitude Practice:

Take a jar and each day place something in the jar you are grateful for. It might be something as small as talking to a friend on the phone, receiving a message from a loved one, seeing the sun shining or feeling fresh air flow through your window. It could include knowing that you are healthy or appreciating the fact that you have more time to complete those projects that you never had the time to complete! Each day, fill the jar with something you are grateful for, then at the end of each week pull out all the slips of paper and read them all together. This is helpful when you need a boost of strength and resilience.

Conclusion

This book provides a road map and several practices which can be applied by anyone who needs to cultivate more resilience during times of loss, grief and uncertainty. I encourage readers to let go of the myths that tell us we must 'stay strong' despite experiencing difficulties and instead welcome all our emotions into us, with a non-judgmental, compassionate awareness. I hope that in applying these practices and by bringing awareness to our process of loss and grief that we will emerge from our crisis with a greater sense of courage, humility and an ability to be vulnerable with ourselves, others and the world. I also feel strongly that it is times of crisis that are the greatest opportunities for us grow and transform psychologically and spiritually.

The book offers us a balance between conscious practices which build our resilience, as well as practices which remind us to trust our process and navigate this time of uncertainty with greater flow and ease. I believe finding this balance between the two is so crucial and if we try to force our way through difficulties without resting in the discomfort, we are in danger of missing out on an opportunity for deeper growth and healing to take place.

As we navigate this uncertain time, some of us may have the chance to step beyond the stories and beliefs which have stopped us from healing in the past. Our journey through loss and grief may also enable us to re-evaluate what is important to us, come into alignment with our core values and connect with a greater meaning and purpose behind all we experience.

For those of us who are experiencing the global coronavirus pandemic 2020, the next stage of our journey will come. We will reach a point where lockdown eases, and we will hopefully start the slow movement into social contact again. However, we cannot be certain what the future holds for us or how our lives will continue to be affected by this pandemic. Our usual routines and ways of being in the world will be irrevocably changed. Some of us will be able to return to our old jobs, others of us will not. Some relationships will have been strengthened through this and there are some relationships which will never be the same again. Yet, it is my hope that despite all this unknown, we will continue to move forward with our lives, using the practices and insights from this book along with the other books in this series. Most importantly we will continue to hold compassion in our hearts for ourselves, each other and the world; staying connected to a deep appreciation and love for the things that are really important to us.

Author's Biography

Jules is a Transpersonal Coach and Therapist who supports people through challenging life transitions and times of crisis. Her focus is to not only help people cultivate resilience through difficulty but to also find meaning and purpose through times of adversity. It is her belief that we are able to emerge through crisis positively transformed.

Over the years Jules has studied various forms of psychology, counselling, mindfulness, coaching and complementary approaches to healing. She holds a BSc in Psychology and an MSc in Transpersonal Psychology, Consciousness and Spirituality and has combined modern day psychology with the teachings from many mystical and spiritual traditions across the world. She lived in Asia for 11 years and has integrated Eastern philosophy and modern day meditation practices into her work. She now lives and works in London, UK where she offers regular sessions and workshops to assist people on their journey towards greater healing and transformation.

Note to Reader

Thank you for purchasing *Resilience: Navigating Loss in a Time of Crisis* I hope that this book serves as a helpful companion on your journey through the path of loss, grief and uncertainty.

If you can, please share a review of the book on your favorite site or the online platform where the book was purchased. If you'd like to stay in touch and find out about my other work, you can visit my website and subscribe to my newsletter on: www.julesdevitto.com. Otherwise, you are welcome to get in touch at: info@julesdevitto.com and follow me on Instagram @ theunboundself. I regularly share articles, posts and much more content on the topics and practices that are mentioned in this book.

Sincerely,

Jules De Vitto

TRANSFORMATION

The *Resilience* Series

The Resilience Series is a collaborative effort by the authors of Changemakers Books in response to the 2020 coronavirus epidemic. Each concise volume offers expert advice and practical exercises for mastering specific skills and abilities. Our intention is that by strengthening your resilience, you can better survive and even thrive in a time of crisis.

Resilience: Adapt and Plan for the New Abnormal of the COVID-19 Coronavirus Pandemic
by Gleb Tsipursky

COVID-19 has demonstrated clearly that businesses, nonprofits, individuals, and governments are terrible at dealing effectively with large-scale disasters that take the form of slow-moving train-wrecks. Using cutting-edge research in cognitive neuroscience and behavioral economics on dangerous judgment errors (cognitive biases), this book first explains why we respond so poorly to slow-moving, high-impact, and long-term crises. Next, the book shares research-based strategies for how organizations and individuals can adapt effectively to the new abnormal of the COVID-19 pandemic and similar disasters. Finally, it shows how to develop an effective strategic plan and make the best major decisions in the context of the uncertainty and ambiguity brought about by COVID-19 and other slow-moving large-scale catastrophes. The author, a cognitive neuroscientist and behavioral economist and CEO of the consulting, coaching, and training firm Disaster Avoidance Experts, combines research-based strategies with real-life stories from his business and nonprofit clients as they adapt to the pandemic.

Resilience: Aging with Vision, Hope and Courage in a Time of Crisis
by John C. Robinson

This book is for those over 65 wrestling with fear, despair, insecurity, and loneliness in these frightening times. A blend of psychology, self-help, and spirituality, it's meant for all who hunger for facts, respect, compassion, and meaningful resources to light their path ahead. The 74-year-old author's goal is to move readers from fear and paralysis to growth and engagement: "Acknowledging the inspiring resilience and wisdom of our hard-won maturity, I invite you on a personal journey of transformation and renewal into a new consciousness and a new world."

Resilience: Connecting with Nature in a Time of Crisis
by Melanie Choukas-Bradley

Nature is one of the best medicines for difficult times. An intimate awareness of the natural world, even within the city, can calm anxieties and help create healthy perspectives. This book will inspire and guide you as you deal with the current crisis, or any personal or worldly distress. The author is a naturalist and certified forest therapy guide who leads nature and forest bathing walks for many organizations in Washington, DC and the American West. Learn from her the Japanese art of "forest bathing": how to tune in to the beauty and wonder around you with all your senses, even if your current sphere is a tree outside the window or a wild backyard. Discover how you can become a backyard naturalist, learning about the trees, wildflowers, birds and animals near your home. Nature immersion during stressful times can bring comfort and joy as well as opportunities for personal growth, expanded vision and transformation.

Resilience: Going Within in a Time of Crisis
by P.T. Mistlberger

During a time of crisis, we are presented with something of a fork in the road; we either look within and examine ourselves, or engage in distractions and go back to sleep. This book is intended to be a companion for men and women dedicated to their inner journey. Written by the author of seven books and founder of several personal growth communities and esoteric schools, each chapter offers different paths for exploring your spiritual frontier: advanced meditation techniques, shadow work, conscious relating, dream work, solo retreats, and more. In traversing these challenging times, let this book be your guide.

Resilience: Grow Stronger in a Time of Crisis
by Linda Ferguson

Many of us have wondered how we would respond in the midst of a crisis. You hope that difficult times could bring out the best in you. Some become stronger, more resilient and more innovative under pressure. You hope that you will too. But you are afraid that crisis may bring out your anxiety, your fears and your weakest communication. No one knows when the crisis will pass and things will get better. That's out of your hands. But *you* can get better. All it takes is an understanding of how human beings function at their best, the willpower to make small changes in perception and behavior, and a vision of a future that is better than today. In the pages of this book, you will learn to create the conditions that allow your best self to show up and make a difference - for you and for others.

Resilience: Handling Anxiety in a Time of Crisis
by George Hofmann

It's a challenging time for people who experience anxiety, and even people who usually don't experience it are finding their moods are getting the better of them. Anxiety hits hard and its symptoms are unmistakable, but sometimes in the rush and confusion of uncertainty we miss those symptoms until it's too late. When things seem to be coming undone, it's still possible to recognize the onset of anxiety and act to prevent the worst of it. The simple steps taught in this book can help you overcome the turmoil.

Resilience: The Life-Saving Skill of Story
by Michelle Auerbach

Storytelling covers every skill we need in a crisis. We need to share information about how to be safe, about how to live together, about what to do and not do. We need to talk about what is going on in ways that keep us from freaking out. We need to change our behavior as a human race to save each other and ourselves. We need to imagine a possible future different from the present and work on how to get there. And we need to do it all without falling apart. This book will help people in any field and any walk of life to become better storytellers and immediately unleash the power to teach, learn, change, soothe, and create community to activate ourselves and the people around us.

Resilience: Navigating Loss in a Time of Crisis
by Jules De Vitto

This book explores the many forms of loss that can happen in times of crisis. These losses can range from loss of business, financial security, routine, structure to the deeper losses of meaning, purpose or identity. The author draws on her background in transpersonal psychology, integrating spiritual insights and mindfulness practices to take the reader on a journey in which to help them navigate the stages of uncertainty that follow loss. The book provides several practical activities, guided visualization and meditations to cultivate greater resilience, courage and strength and also explores the potential to find greater meaning and purpose through times of crisis.

Resilience: Virtually Speaking
Communicating at a Distance
by Teresa Erickson and Tim Ward

To adapt to a world where you can't meet face-to-face – with air travel and conferences cancelled, teams working from home – leaders, experts, managers and professionals all need to master the skills of virtual communication. Written by the authors of *The Master Communicator's Handbook*, this book tells you how to create impact with your on-screen presence, use powerful language to motivate listening, and design compelling visuals. You will also learn techniques to prevent your audience from losing attention, to keep them engaged from start to finish, and to create a lasting impact.

Resilience: Virtual Teams
Holding the Center When You Can't Meet Face-to-Face
by Carlos Valdes-Dapena

In the face of the COVID-19 virus organizations large and small are shuttering offices and factories, requiring as much work as possible be done from people's homes. The book draws on the insights of the author's earlier book, *Lessons from Mars*, providing a set of the powerful tools and exercises developed within the

Mars Corporation to create high performance teams. These tools have been adapted for teams suddenly forced to work apart, in many cases for the first time. These simple secrets and tested techniques have been used by thousands of teams who know that creating a foundation of team identity and shared meaning makes them resilient, even in a time of crisis.